1-5-11

Dear Paul +
Suzanne-
Thank you so much
for your true
support

I truly appreciate
Best of luck with everything

Love + Friendship

Intuition
The Ultimate Unity

(Unedited)

a Collaboration of
Fantasy and Reality
Inspired Poems
with Photo Art

Nicole Cavaluzzi

authorHOUSE®

AuthorHouse™
1663 Liberty Drive
Bloomington, IN 47403
www.authorhouse.com
Phone: 1-800-839-8640

First published by AuthorHouse 8/22/2011

ISBN: 978-1-4634-3738-1 (e)
ISBN: 978-1-4634-3736-7 (hc)
ISBN: 978-1-4634-3737-4 (sc)

Library of Congress Control Number: 2011913005

Printed in the United States of America

This book is printed on acid-free paper.

Because of the dynamic nature of the Internet, any web addresses or links contained
in this book may have changed since publication and may no longer be valid. The views
expressed in this work are solely those of the author and do not necessarily reflect the
views of the publisher, and the publisher hereby disclaims any responsibility for them.

authorHOUSE has allowed this work to remain exactly as the
author intended, verbatim, without editorial input.

Warning–Disclaimer

Every effort has been made to make this poetry book of fiction complete and accurate as possible. However, there *may be mistakes*, both typographical and in content.

Parental Advisory Warning–This poetry book may be inappropriate for children due to brief sexual content and violent language.

This text should not be used as a general guide. The purpose of the poems and art in this book is to entertain. The author and publishing company shall have neither liability nor responsibility to any person or entity with respect to any loss or damage caused or alleged to have been caused, or actions caused, or alleged to have been caused or done directly or indirectly, by the information contained in this book.

By purchasing this poetry book you are bound by the above.

Other writings by Nicole Cavaluzzi:

A poetry book:
Titled: **Must Have Been Those Butterflies**
A Collaboration of Lust, Infatuation, and Love
Inspired Poems with Photo Art

An autobiography (currently underway, available Spring 2012):
Titled: **Love: Denied!**

INTUITION, THE ULTIMATE UNITY is a collaboration of fantasy and reality inspired poems with photo art.

My best intention to open the minds and touch the souls with words and images created from my personal experiences exploring the magical wonders of the human psyche ...interchanging fantasies and realities.

I share my words and images in hope to intrigue the reader to embrace and interchange within themselves: Fantasies, realities, thoughts, dreams, visions, feelings and reactions.

Anything and everything is possible inside one's mind. Follow one's intuition; enable one's fantasies to transcend into realities: Experience the Ultimate Unity.

I vow to always believe in the possibility of the ultimate unity of fantasy and reality, as I follow mine: Intuition.

In Loving Memory of
My Friends and Family
Who Have Passed On...

"Missing You Reminds Me,
Your Essence is Always With Me,
An Angel Watching Over Me,
Your Resting Soul Inspires Me..."

Love, Light and Happiness, Nicole

~Contents~

~Fantasy or Reality?~

~Fantasy~

~Reality~

~Transition from Fantasy to Reality~

~Union of Fantasy and Reality~

*"There are no imperfections in poetry...
only challenging perspectives."
~Nicole Cavaluzzi~*

~Fantasy or Reality?~

"Illusions of the mind may just be confusion in a world refined."

Subconscious or Ego?

Paradox

The need to grasp
what is not here,
elements desired,
yet so unclear.
No images
of what I seek,
no concept,
dull mind bleak.
A dream
does not exist,
for what I want,
yet do not miss.
What then
can it be?
from these eyes,
I do not see.
Temptations to have
what I do not know,
then is it,
where I cannot go?
Curiosity
taunts my hunger,
my mind cannot sleep,
upon this blunder.
The only thing
that can be done,
is to wait,
for what may never come.

Apology

What, exactly, is going on?
Sometimes I feel like everything's wrong.
Emotional outbreaks, nerves forcing tears,
Love is an obstacle that has many fears.

The start of a relationship brings on joy,
But seriousness: a mind's toy.
Multiple selves battle within,
Loving-self counteracts hating-self -no one wins.

There's no true solution to a catch twenty-two,
The never ending disillusion of don't and do.
Stress compliments moments of rage,
Words misspoken, destroys my self image.

What can one do when it's down to that moment?
The moment when one knows there's a need to connect.
Misspoken words must untangle,
The voice of anger subsides, conflicts unmangle.

So when it is time to apologize,
I'll take back the cruel tones, mellow the vibes.
For now, I can only think to say one thing:
It's not my fault for being me, blame me for what's within.

Living Hurts

Please Lord, kill me now
My pain is so deep, I cannot survive
This life of agony, I dread
I no longer want to be alive

My life has fallen to pieces
I am apathetic to all I know
Give me a way to escape
I will gladly take it and go

I hate this feeling
I just want to die and never wake
My depression is overwhelming
This constant pressure I cannot take

Lift me into the clouds
Or drop me to the hells below
It doesn't matter to me
Whichever way I deserve to go

Just get me out of here
This life I cannot continue to live
I have no hope for fate
Nothing I have is worth to give

I just take up space
On this planet we call Earth
Stab me, shoot me, do something
I feel no pain, but living hurts

There is no loss in the matter
I'm sure no one will mind
I would be happier dead
I am a failure to all mankind

I really hate myself
Knowing I am worthless to all
Please kill me, my Lord
And let my lifeless body fall

Self Pity

Fading into my mind's black hole,
Feelings emerging I can't control.
Sadness lurking, I'm drowning in tears,
Self pity infects me, an overwhelming fear.
Choking on an addiction of self infliction,
Chugging on a reaction, denying satisfaction.
Calculating ways to increase the tension,
Manipulating thoughts for the ultimate melt-down.

Numerous excuses enhancing self abuses,
My self tormenting transmitters burning fuses.
A scrape will not scar but will tear me apart,
Extending my self induced pain ever so far.
Effort to ensure my life has been scorned,
A lonely world inside my mind forever endured.
Finding my head in a split post internal fits,
Pursuing self destruction: Wanting what I cannot get.

Alone, Crazy, Bored

Alone
In this haunted cell;
My mind enslaved
To this place I dwell.

Crazy
I twitch, do not touch;
My body consumed
Paranoia has struck.

Bored
I am restless, expired;
My heart drained
This life I retire.

Becomes of You, Insane

Your like the violet blood,
That runs through my veins:

Exposed to air,
Turning red;
Becomes of you, Insane.

A flash of black,
In those evil eyes,
Now stare into the fires below:

You know that your a sinner,
And that is where you'll go.

Love or Pain?

He and She

He admires Her:
charisma
charm
character
& Karma...

She admires His:
appeal
allure
happiness
& zeal...

He provides Her:
ecstasy
fantasy
mystery
& chemistry...

She provides Him:
safety
security
reality
& destiny...

He describes Her:
psychotic
neurotic
erotic
& manic...

She describes Him:
crazy
lazy
sexy
& dizzy...

He denies Her:
loyalty
honesty
harmony
& sympathy...

She denies Him:
sanity
stability
serenity
& pity...

He burns Her
She scorns Him...
He hurts Her
She ignores Him...

He loves Her
She yearns Him...
He lures Her
She falls for Him...

Alas, the cycle starts all over again.

Comforts Collide

lost in a memory
climax of love
happiness, blissfulness
my soul mate, the one

always extreme
no in between
my passionate lover
man of my dreams

heart in a flutter
butterfly net
no other exists
his love a sure bet

him loving me
unexplainable joy
no words describe
the love we employed

alas, a memory
no longer my life
a disagreement
love we sacrificed

to carry on
a challenge each day
we decide it's best
to go separate ways

never the same page
comforts collide
with strong love
comes love suicide

passionate lovers
hurt driven deep
destroying dreams
no longer sleep

a sad memory
of passion missed
replacement impossible
for the one I can't resist

Manic

In my dreams he coddles me,
But a stranger in reality.
In my heart, can't set him free,
Our love lives on in fantasy.

Reality of his love: a nightmare,
Taunted by his true demeanor.
Driving me to manic episodes,
Delusions, paranoia, psychosis; overload!

Who is this stranger who tortures me?
Who am I to let him treat me so badly?
No respect, nor consideration,
He can't relate to my manic frustrations.

Alas, I blame myself for loving him,
To fall for a rebel, one cannot win.
My manic mind, forever tormented,
Greiving loss; fate dormanted.

Opposites Attract

Laying,
Wondering,
Loving,
Suffering.

Smiling,
Wailing,
Stifling,
Draining.

In concert,
Apart,
Magnets,
Separate.

Recalling,
Denying,
Reminiscing,
Contradicting.

Adored,
Abhorred,
Loved,
Loathed.

Loyal,
Rival,
Be all,
Foe.

Patience

Gypsy on a journey,
No time to belong,
Searching for his destiny,
Striving to stay strong.

Neurotic lover sits,
Impatiently awaiting him,
She desperately longs his kiss,
Alone, she can't go on.

Opposites, dreams collide,
She cries at night,
He wonders the world,
Love, interrupted, by time.

Struggling to hang on,
Feeling lucky to be alive,
She knows she must go on,
Fighting the odds to survive.

His words promise hope,
His actions absent of love,
On her words she chokes,
But she refuses to move on.

Her heart tells her to wait,
Her mind screams for freedom,
A prisoner of her own fate,
Alas, she cannot leave him.

Sober or Altered State?

Drunk

Spinning vigorously
Around, around, around,
Prespiring heavily
Bare feet slap the ground.
Dialating pupils
Vision's disturbed,
Voices mock me
Can't comprehend words.
Feeling fatigue
Mingling body falls numb,
Clammy hands grab
Another shot of rum.
Dancing obnoxiously
I am the star of the show,
Fellas join me
Viscious wives bellow.
Too tired to fight
I seek refuge for the night,
Awake in a fugue state
Hazy memories
Recall drunk mistakes.

'e'

they say the first time is always the best
a feeling arouses that's greater than sex
the future looks brighter than ever before
your nemesis is no more
everything is loud and clear
your body clings to whomever is near
you are the happiest person alive
everyone should try this adrenaline drive
but at the point you feel your stomach drop
and it feels like the fun is going to stop
remember friends will go far
to lift you back up to where you were

high

drifting my lazy eyes
around this room of discovery
aroma of incense arises
unconscious mind begins wondering
my thoughts amaze me
as I lay here in a state of confusion
the radio becomes a setting
images of dancing feet amuse me
I try to move my lips
but my throat is barren
cannot release vocals
this numbness that has overcome me
tingling my toes
crumpling my brain
falling into a never ending sleep
feels so good to shut my lids
dreaming of meadows with daisies and violets
smiling at my own jokes
I cry when I feel pain
becoming mad because nothing has gone my way
thankful to finally awake
dazed I realize I am fine
except for this lingering headache
finding myself I roll light and smoke again
beginning another trip into my world of discoveries

Beginning or Ending?

For One Sad Moment

Cold and crowded
came darkness
confusion pursued it destiny
sadness lured into dreams
answers were deceased
time was put aside
the day he died.

Fog and clouds
shadows unknown
voices linger as background noise
patience does not exist
faces of stone
no one is real
remorse is all they feel.

Rain pours with anger
happiness is not found within
a whisper would break the silence
now thick in the air
faith has not yet surfaced
within the heart conceals what is known
only a solid sigh is shown.

With Hope

I see a vision
that won't come clear,
I listen close
but cannot hear.   .

I feel the hurt
that pride won't show,
I taste the pain
but cannot know.

I dream of souls
that won't give in,
I try to help
but cannot begin.

I have a heart
that wants to understand,
I try to care
but cannot comprehend.

I pity the victims
who won't open to me,
I cry for them
but cannot bare empathy.

Requiem I

Blaze of darkness;
Thick in the air,
As we enter this mortal phenomenon.
Transfixed;
Morose, sullen thoughts,
Light requiem reposing our loved ones.

Requiem II

Shedding tears of torment;
Spoiled face,
Hazy view.
Sighs of pain in vain,
I must accept,
His death was due.

Aching unfathomable sorrow,
I grieve;
So deep.
Anguish burns my heart,
Selfishly,
I somberly weep.

Black rings invade my eyes,
No desire,
Sleep deprived.
Self pity for he who died,
Oh Requiem,
Silence my cries!

A New Way

Day breaks
I am lost
In this place
Where I once felt whole,
No longer safe.

It was they
Whose denial
Drove him to stay
He refused to live a lie,
Enforced a new way.

It was he
Who cried
Sins so free
A fool's confession,
Mercy for destiny.

It is here
I recall
He disappeared
His lingering scent,
Strong with fear.

When dusk did fall
I searched
All night long
A desperate attempt,
Alas, he is gone.

~Fantasy~

"Beautiful, happy, lustful destiny! Alas, beware, the dangerous counter-balance that must be..."

Inspired From Within

Falling rain
Downpours define
Thoughts that ponder
Never enough time
Broken windows
Barriers so fine
Battles within
Longing to shine

Winds whirling
Spinning chimes
Theories stirring
My restless mind
Notions turning
Looking to find
Blazes burning
Inspiring design

Thunder drones
Drowning ideas
Ego on hold
Subconscious gears
Ever so bold
Superior spear
Taking control
I express my fears

Seasons (of My Life)

Each fresh, sweet new day,
Heals my heart from yesterday.
Sunshine steers my mind from harping,
Serene snow slows my thoughts from churning.

Fall breeze, crisp, sets me free,
Sprinkling rain defines my will to be.
Shadowing clouds hide the days of cold,
Warming fire, deep within my soul.

Thundering storms suddenly scream,
Lightening strikes: A streak so mean.
Hail denies a peaceful path,
Flooding rivers bring back my past.

Winds whip, my words are sick,
Tears in my eyes, but my skin is thick.
Tornados torture my broken spirit,
Hurricanes tire me, I cannot repeat it!

Alas, soft sunlight sets me at ease,
Sand on my feet, waves relaxing me.
The silence of a sunset beach soothes,
Seasons of my life; an ever-changing groove.

Coming of the Truth

with pride
wide-eyed
narrow-minded
wicked smile
his teeth shining
the light was in his hands
in the dark
they were amazed
the waves of light
how quick his wrist
did switch
the powerful sticks
about his own body
they stared either
jealous and envious
or with delight and approval
the creation of reality infers
the truth is evil

Subliminal Torture

Subliminally, he tortures me,
Love slave; infatuated by his mystery.
Dangling emotions, he enforces my devotion,
His taunting corroborates his seductive action.

I open my heart to let love in,
Yet, I attract a life of infatuation.
Basis: sexual chemistry, lust on fire,
Mistaken for love; object of his desire.

He lures me into his sexual world,
I bow to him and everything he does.
Prisoner of his love, I am at his beck and call,
Embarrassed, ashamed, a victim of love I fall.

Chain around my neck, lock on my heart,
Handcuffs and a whip, no option to part.
He controls me with his wicked ways,
His passion draws me in, I can't escape.

It's Begun

Nervously, I move towards you,
Kiss your lips, it's all brand new.
Feel the rhythm of your heart,
Subdued, I play the part.

Slow motion, fast ride,
Into you, I slide.
Your scent takes me away,
I taste you, we begin to play.

Curiously, I let you seduce me,
You breathe down my neck, warmly.
Your bite entices, I'm so alive,
I pull you close, let you pry.

Want you now, take me hard,
Go to places, close and far.
Feel my lust, strong for you,
My heart pounds, I can't say no.

Your eyes tell me, it's time,
I hold you tight, start to cry.
Passion leads me, climax near,
When I'm with you, I have no fear.

In this moment, I share with you,
There is no end, forever I do.
Connection runs deep, I'm falling in love,
Lie in your arms, and know it's begun.

Sultry Love

Wild, radiant essence,
Blazing with desire,
Melting satin sheets,
Insatiable, on fire.

Avid, passionate romance,
Burning so fervent,
Warming hearts meld,
Inseparable, love ardent.

Fiery, zealous legend,
Sizzling in lust,
Heating spirits rise,
Intense, hot thrust.

Deep, devoted souls,
Smoking, sultry love,
Scorching ardor reigns,
Ignition of flames is us.

Sober or Altered State?

Murderer

Igniting sparks flash in dry air,
Reflection: Fantasy or nightmare?
Flaming fires melt the ice,
Contemplation: The irony of life.

Drowning in a flood of confusion;
Deliberation: Reality or illusion?
Burning with flashbacks: Revolting imagery,
Observation: Am I really she?

Fantasy of a handsome face,
Nightmare of a long forgotten place.
Ironic moment as he held me down,
My life I had to save, and so it began...

Reality of me, a woman in despair,
Recall now- a body behind the stair.
Vivid flashbacks of brutality,
Remembering now-more than one fatality...

Illusions of a bloody, rusty ax,
Psychosis took over me, when he attacked.
A victim's vengeance, oh what had I done?
A snowball effect to maintain my freedom.

Flashbacks haunt my tainted mind,
This blood on my hands, I still deny.
A murderer? I am not she!
But the truth...will always lie within me.

Vampire Feeds

Keen swords
Sink through
Thick flesh
Drawing blood
Tasty sour violet
Stain my lips
My buds feel
The familiar suds
Seeping...
Erotic wild eyes
Excitement by moonlight
Seeking to quench
Insatiable hunger
Devouring another
Kiss of death
Smooth and satisfying
Ravenous desire
Lusting...
Spread wings
Night cap time
Morning brings
Bright sun
On the horizon
Mortal moon
Now hiding
Rest until the next
Moon rising...

Heroine

With unconditional passion
Arises a heroine,
Destined to save him
From nature's sins.

Her strength is from within
Focus is on survival,
Heated fire rising
Her destiny does call.

She pushes through
Thickened soot, black ash,
Risks her own life
Rescues him from darkness.

She handles him delicately
Coddling, protecting,
Acting on instinct
Never neglecting him.

A heroine has risen
Her colors shine through,
She puts his life before her own
As a true heroine would do.

Beginning or Ending?

Victim to Be

A blindfold conceals my eyes;
Vision's thick,
Tears run dry.
Stomach knotted, oh so sick!
Where am I? What time is it?!

A substance drips on my tear stained cheek;
Startling me,
Deeming me weak.
Insecurities rapidly increase,
It's past my bedtime, uneasiness creeps.

A hand holds mine and squeezes tight;
Pain tingling torture,
I try to fight.
Pathetic, I fail, tender, sore,
Midnight falls, this fear I can't ignore!

A wet slimy tongue, cold upon my lips;
Vile breath,
Talks of whips.
Whispers of ghastly threats,
It must be 2 am, where are my parents?!

A haunting noise pierces-oh how I wish I could forget!
Sudden cool draft,
Footsteps fade in fret.
I scream aloud, hopelessly, for help,
Morning is coming, someone must be on the look out?!

A psychopath, no conscious to barter;
He's killing me!
Soulless monster.
I am his victim, and soon to be: history,
In awe, I realize, I'm just another casualty.

Sniper

A heart beats: rapidly, repetitiously,
A voice murmurs: softly, meticulously.
Lingering in the stillness of the night:
Waiting, anticipation,
An urge he can't fight.
An ear listens: keenly, cautiously,
A palm sweats: tightly, nervously.
Clutched on the trigger of the pistol:
A hand so large it holds more than a fistful.
A shadow is still: slyly, silently,
A nose inhales: strongly, confidently.
A sound is heard:
Although it's mild,
The sniper attacks an innocent child.

Nightmare

Each dreadful night as I lay in bed,
Morbid thoughts fill my anxious head.
Serpents scrape sadistically at my door,
Creatures lurk ferociously upon my floor.
Venemous shrills and screams pitch so high,
Satan laughs fiercely at my silent cries.
Chains clasp tightly around my bleeding wrists,
This never-ending nightmare I must resist!
Alas, my conscious refuses to let me wake,
My swollen eyes cursed, vision now opaque.
All that my sorely abused eyes cannot see,
Doesn't stop my mind from churning gorey imagery.
Tired of fighting a hopeless struggle I withdraw,
Evil takes over, my state of mind: obscure.
Ambiguously damned to a grim, clammy cell,
Vile hostility surrounds me, I'm a prisoner of Hell.

Hell

Drops of blood rapidly fall
Cries from souls tortured, mauled
Hearts of sorrow say their prayers
Those damned to Hell must do their share
Hot coals burn their sacred feet
Scorned sinners trapped in Satan's heat
To earn reverence of all below
They must learn Evil's call
Bleeding in their time of pain
They must suffer to understand
Chosen by He who has brought them here
To learn to love the way of fear

Gates of Hell

Inspire me to tell a tale
Of demons and serpents
And the places they dwell:
A world of death pits;
Cold, damp, darkness,
Stench of death decay,
Viscious screams of victims preyed.
Blood curdling devils,
And monsters of the sort,
Dare enter the Gates of Hell,
It will be your last resort.

No Escape

Mysterious, cold hands
Touching my face,
Virgin body held captive
A victim in a wicked place.

Trembling uncontrollably
I hold back my shrills,
Evil darkess laughs aloud
His ecstasy longing to kill.

Knowing death is approaching
Bloody imagery takes a hold,
I have no say in this sacrfice
This evil presence has my soul.

4th Kind

Bloody shrills
so keen;
penetrate my brainwashed mind.

Nimble shadows
so obscene;
nothing of the human kind.

My Twisted Hiaku

A silver shimmer
Catches the unaware eye
Machete attacks

~Reality~

"Good, bad or indifferent, reality is the genuine result, even if we don't recognize it."

Subconscious or Ego?

Rock Bottom

Dream big,
Fall hard,
Blind fate,
Loss of love.

No words,
Dull emotions,
Numb heart,
Null of devotion.

Pending fame,
All in vain,
Make-up smeared,
Exposed shame.

Drama now,
Spiral down,
Toll taken,
Tragic frown.

Ego, No More

A once protective shield collapses,
Delicate walls gently crumble.
Words of truth, no retraction,
Raw exposure, brutally humble.

A mask used to save face cracks,
Bridges drawn forced apart.
Ignorant mind, derails off tracks,
Shock waves compel an honest heart.

Beneath the surface of ugly ego,
Melting ice washing away.
Lies the truth, crackling through,
A reality denied, a life on display.

Limelight shines down into the core,
Of the inner being self assured.
Timid calmness, graces allure,
This is who I am, ego no more.

an end...

my heart is in my hands
this hurt i cannot comprehend
this gripping pain won't let me be
anger fueled frustration
taking over me

i want to cry, to scream
to runaway, to live a dream
the hate i feel has no name
this emptiness
is all in vain

my spirit has completely died
my happiness has withered dry
there's nothing left for me to love
i've tried everything
to want to live

this life has led me to an end
i can't go on, i can't amend
there is no meaning in this world
my bleeding heart
has lost morale

my eyes have seen enough
i seek refuge from distrust
to rest in peace, i chose to cease
goodnight cruelty
goodbye beast

High Sensitivity

Profile me!
Go ahead, come n' see
A dirty girl,
An ugly mystery...
Scope me!
Inside, diseased
A broken doll,
A pathetic lil tease...
Enslave me!
Alone, but never free
A lost loner,
A soul without destiny...
Capture me!
Jaded, fallen desperately
A beggar now,
Foolishly, a slave to thee...
Torture me!
Alive, I die slowly
Dense eyes,
Blind now, he's all I see...
Forgive me!
My high sensitivity
Tear stained smile,
Love takes control of me.

Dissolved

Once in time
Faces so pure,
Innocent flesh was scorned.
Time and it's moments
No longer form,
A place once known
Now torn.

Peaceful with fate
Not a care for fear,
Betrayal dominates atmosphere.
Ignorant minds
Bleed in their hearts,
The place they live
They must depart.

Cannot recall time
When life was gay,
Dissolved by outbreak of envy.
A place once loved
Now absent of sense,
No longer fancied
Just burning resentment.

My True Colors

I sit and watch the days go by,
Nothing seems to affect me.
To think that life could hurt so bad,
I wish that I could never be.

No one can understand my side,
I see things...differently.
When I can sense how others feel,
I know that they repulse me.

To recognize that I am no one special,
Turns me into someone else.
Saving face, I pretend I am fine,
So no one, but me, will see my real self.

Depression always sheds a tear,
I don't know the reasons I cry.
But to know that there's nothing for me,
I think of how I want to die.

One will ask questions, in sympathy,
Ask what's wrong with no idea.
I cannot explain why I feel this way,
Nothing I can tell for anyone to hear.

So now I end the story of my life,
My true colors have been shown.
Anyone who actually understands me,
I wouldn't have thought you'd have known.

Covert

Time is halted
as he is haunted
by a perfect stranger
he calls "a friend".
A spoken word
a friendly gesture
nothing is heard
about what she is after.

She closes her doors
shuts others out
except for he
who offers what he's about.
He will give
and she'll take him for granted
for all he is worth
her vision is slanted.

The pleasure she seeks
is covert greed
takes all she can get
until he starts to bleed.
This tragic turning point
dark elegies of remorse
twists her moral soul
she is the murderer of the source.

Confessing unforgivable sins
she is unsuccessful
her scars of hidden pain exposed
her epistemology is frightful.
Attempting to forget her regretful ways
she cries tears of denial
he cannot forgive her covert deciet
alas, her life is on trial.

empty

dreams a blur
thoughts a stir
fantasies gone
life is done
hopes vanish
beliefs scatter
psyche bored
life is scorned
laughter silent
cries quiet
destiny drowned
life is unknown
words withdrawn
voice worn
spirit un-kind
life is led blind
feelings numb
mind dumb
true-self dies
life is a lie

A Life of Nothing

A life of nothing
Is a life without meaning:
Smile fading slowly away
Remains of disaster and decay.
Buried deep in perpetual hurt
Pleading soul, desperate to find worth.

A life of nothing
Is a life without dreaming:
Damaged, broken down
Crooked face, permenant frown.
Beneath, defeated, living low,
In dark places emptiness grows.

A life of nothing
Is a life without believing:
Can't remember, realms erased
Gave up, too many mistakes.
Shallow mind, unable to relate
Forgetting all, undetermined fate.

A life is nothing:
Without meaning
Without dreaming
Without believing
Alas, "Without" demeans
Life.

Lucky Me

Torture chamber is the perfect way
To describe my life, from day to day.
Work and school and chores and bills,
Ex-boyfriends don't clean up their spills.
Matters worsen, I start cursing,
Time is an essence that I dismay.

The perfect face I shall maintain
As migraines run through my brain.
If I look, it's right through you,
A solid stare will stick like glue.
Matters worsen, I start cursing,
Time is an essence that I restrain.

The aura that my skin releases
Body temperature constantly increases.
My touch is like a burning match,
I'll scorch you if you turn your back.
Matters worsen, I start cursing,
Time is an essence I wish would cease.

Sleep is not an easy method
Sheep and dogs I give no credit.
Toss and turn til dawn is come,
The rising sun, just feels wrong.
Matters worsen, I start cursing,
Time is an essence I give no acceptance.

What to do I'll never know
My illness is from head to toe,
Mind is churning, yet not working,
Matters worsen, I can't stop cursing,
Time is an essence I'll never know.

Love or Pain?

Lost Soul

He swears his love is genuine,
Yet he can't seem to give me time.
He's focused on being a man,
So he can't be distracted by a woman.

He pleads his words speak truth,
But his attitude screams aloof.
He denies being a player,
How can I trust him? little liar.

A lost soul, who simply cannot love,
Alas, the man has not grown up.
Arrested development, he doesn't get it,
No matter how many times I explain it.

He offers me nothing but heartache,
This lost soul, his ways I cannot tolerate.
Backburner every time I give in,
I subject myself glutton to his life of sin.

I must run fast, and far away,
He lures me in with his charming way.
He's easy to love when he's in my arms,
A passionate lover he glistens with charm.

This man has stolen my heart,
Thief of love, a lost soul can't be fought.
I must blame myself for being a fool,
He's captured my soul, now lost, lost soul.

One Mean Bitch

I can't tell you
How I feel
You're a closed book-
Love doesn't appeal.
Your eyes are dark
Your heart is black
You're sooo cold!
You're a heart attack!
You're the darkest man
I've ever met-
Stole my heart
Never gave it back!
And now
I am one mean bitch
Hate on men
Don't put up with shit
And now
Your new bitch
Has to deal with you
And all your shit!
Your evil ways
Catch up with you
Your no good lies
Don't cover the truth
You work so hard
To be such a dick
But the ladies catch on
We won't put up with it
And now
I am one mean bitch
Hate on men
Don't put up with shit

Passion Lost

Why am I sitting here
down in the dumps?
Why am I wasting time
being in a slump?
There are so many things
I could be doing!
Problem is,
I'm tied down by my feelings.

When I'm on top of the world
and life is great,
a broken heart
takes it all away.
Where is my passion
I have for my talents?
Alas, I lost my drive
when he dug in his talons.

And now I,
I just sit here,
And I,
I have no ambition
to get back my passion.
It's my passion
I'm missing now.

Why do I let a man
take away my power?
How can one person
make me such a downer?
I have so many friends
that I could be seeing!
Problem is,
I know I should be relieving.

When you fall in love
nothing else matters.
When you lose that love
your whole world shatters.
Where is the passion
that has made me who I am?
How can this happen
when I am better off without him?

And now I,
I just sit here,
And I,
I have no ambition
to get back my passion.
It's my passion
I'm missing now.

So come
give me that push,
I need a good look!
A reminder of who I am:
A passionate girl.

And now I,
I can't just sit here,
And I,
I must be steered
to get my head cleared.
It's my passion
I'm in need of embracing now.

Break up

Fighting a fever
Maneuver my deceiver,
Feeling his guilt
Shriveled...I wilt.

Pushing for purity
Clarity for uncertainties,
Shedding his deceit
Defeated...I am weak.

Straining for sanity
Vanity is reality,
Exposing his secret
Mistakes...I regret.

Hoping for humbleness
Forgiveness in feebleness,
Releasing his heart
Broken...we part.

If Love is Not the Answer

His heart once warm
Genuine, kind
But his priorities lacking-
Would they change in time?

A love behind doors
Perfect every night
But a public display-
Recipe for a fight.

The hurtful words
The pain incurred
Damages done-
My lover now gone.

Trying to figure out
How to move on
If love is not the answer-
How do I carry on?

Missing Him

Complicated heart can't decide
When to love, when to hide.
Where to go, days of cold
How to sleep...feelings not told.

Troubled mind can't forgive
Want to go, but missing him.
Need to live, must move on
Tied to him...thus so alone.

Lost soul can't escape
What to do, another mistake.
Let me out, search release
Trapped in love...can't breathe.

Sad eyes can't say goodbye
Wanting him, endless cry.
Save me now, help me see
Memories of him...consume me.

No Matter How Much, You Lose

No matter, how big your heart,
Someone always comes and rips it apart.
Especially, when you bend over backwards,
The more you enable, the more it burns.

No matter, how beautiful your face,
Someone always prettier to take your place.
Especially, when you are considerate and sweet,
The more you give, the more he cheats.

No matter, how you adjust your life,
Someone always more carefree and alive.
Especially, when you go out of your way,
The more you do, the more he takes away.

No matter, how you sacrifice your time,
Someone always better than you, more in line.
Especially, when you drive miles on end,
The more mileage, the more he's just a friend.

No matter, how many tears you cry,
Someone else is in his heart, she doesn't even try.
Especially, when you share your heart,
In the end, you always get hurt.

Poison

How do I make it go away?
I just don't know how!
How do I rid this poison?
Poison addiction that feeds my soul...

This serpent he slithered
With scales on his back,
Slime in the flesh;
Ruthless razors in effect...

Satan in sheep's clothing
Charm hypnotized my lonely heart,
Although, never a rose-
Sexual tension he always brought.

Sucking my soul of life
His venom controlled me,
Hopeless I fell for
A snake without loyalty.

He tampered with trust
My lover was a monster,
His evil poison cursed me
My heart a jaded failure.

Rememberance

Although I know it's taboo,
My heart misses you, so much,
I bathe myself in tears,
Yearning for your touch.

Your fingers entangled in mine,
Giggling at each other's jokes,
Our bodies wrapped; unison,
Sharing kisses, loving strokes.

I dream of the great memories of us,
Recall your promise to love me, always,
Wondering now, how you let me go,
Regretting losing you, not understanding how.

Why can't our love live on?
So powerful, the emotions it drives,
Does pride really mean that much to you?
How could we not give it another try?

Alas, our noses held high,
Stubborn heads, neither will budge,
Everything that we enveloped together,
Destroyed, by our ill-fated love.

Anti-Valentine

Sadness soaks her fragile face,
Poignant dreams,
Big mistakes.
Regret from her heart,
So sorely it aches,
Won't justify mercy;
He clutches unwavering hate.

It's not pride, nor dignity,
But a desolate urge,
For sympathy.
She prays for pity,
Embracing faith,
She grasps the last of her grace;
He denies her with distaste.

Her heart encompasses blame,
Desperate wounds,
Full of shame.
Searching for solace,
Yearning forgiveness,
She practices romance;
He rejects her with vengeance.

In despair she presses on,
Trying in vain,
His love is gone.
Suffering in solitude,
Pouting her pathetic tune,
She gives in to go down;
He crushed her in her failed pursuit.

Impossible

A second chance
At chemical romance,
Passion at last
We cannot resist!
Alas, our connection
A love of tension,
With true intentions
Yet many apprehensions:
Dishonest truths
Jealous accusations,
Attitudes aloof
Fevered frustrations...
Chords struck
Thus love, we gave up,
Hurting too much
To make it work.
Stranded...missing you,
Pain, I cannot break through,
Our love: Undeniable!
But undeniably: Impossible!

Tied to Love

Ties we share
They keep us here
In love when near
I gasp for air

The sight of you
Love once true
A past returns
Old but new

You are you
And I, me
Past lovers
Tied by family

Can't deny
Our hearts do tie
Yet circumstance
Won't let us bind

What was once
Just can't be
Tied to love
We must set free

Please Tell Me

How do I stop hurting?
I know I can't give in,
Knowing he's still alive
But I am dead to him.
How can he move forward?
Pretend I don't exist,
Yet, I cry endlessly!
I just cannot accept
That we will never be,
My heart just won't let me
Move on to a new love,
He's all I ever think of.
How do I go on like this?
Sobbing every day...
No matter how busy I am,
Always something reminds me.
It just doesn't feel right
To move on with my life,
I know that he's the one
That I'll grow old with in time.
So I'd just like to tell him
As I am hopeless within,
The one who stole my heart
The only one who I'd ever thought
Would look into my eyes
And make me his bride...
I plead, as I swallow my pride:

My dear love, the only one,
Please tell me what to do!
Why deny a love that's true?
I can't breathe without you...

Sober or Altered State?

Sober

Sober is the way of the lonely one,
Amongst friends, I stand alone.
In the corner I can't help to judge,
Annoyed by the laughter, I once absorbed.

A stranger to myself,
I can't seem to find justice,
No tolerance, cannot sustain the party,
Humble, yet I feel like I lost a part of me.

Once a girl with no limits,
Now a woman with no patience.
Love the new me, but cannot relate,
To a life I once loved, the people in it.

Struggle with my new life,
Sober living just doesn't feel right.
Ignorant to what this could mean for me,
I hang on to a life I miss beyond belief.

Others

They seemed so innocent
At first glance,
But when I got to know them
My feelings advanced.

They were just like me
Enjoyed the same things,
But when I found them out
My thoughts clinged.

Were they worse than I?
Probably, by much,
Their stories were unreal
With a fibby touch.

They spoke about sex
And common gossip,
When they spoke their stories
None had a concept.

I realized soon enough
That I was right,
Their lies were insane
Exaggerated, out of sight.

Their words burned me
Inside and out,
So I turned my head
And walked about.

A Prayer

I am afraid of what I have done;
I have sinned so wrongly against God's word.
What I now confess, may be noise to your ears,
But I have seen the light, and I must be heard.

I love my soul mate and understand our vow,
Yet in the past I hurt him, so he needs to hear me now.
I want to say I am sorry, and that he is all I need,
I know apologies are too late, when all I can do is plead.

I have crossed many lines and tested someone's life,
See now I know what I want, but it doesn't make it right.
I want to be cleansed of this worn soul of sin,
A reborn woman with a need to believe from within.

If I can make things real and start over again,
This foolish world could not manipulate me to sin.

A Gift of Irony

This is the way
Love always ends
Neurotic psychosis
Leaves me alone again.

The pain hides
Raw heart numb
Swallow pills to
Forget his love's gone.

Live life knowing
Senses show me
The truth behind lies
I wish I couldn't see.

Too wise to deny
Realities shine
A gift of irony
A world inside my mind.

A lonely girl
In an isolated place
Love always lost
Emotions aroused erased.

Sober mind
Living for honesty
Sorry broken heart
Certainty forever haunting me.

Dead Beat

Going crazy, Smokin' bones
So damn lazy, Gettin' stoned

Ignore life, Just don't care
Reality bites, Just can't bare

Cry alone, Laugh too
No one home, Nothin' to do

Dread love, Roses die
No dove, In my sky

Blood crawls, Fingers numb
Stare at walls, Lookin' dumb

Beat the blues, Still not here
Can't refuse, Another beer

Closed doors, Bed is made
Not a looker, Ain't gettin' laid

A dead beat, Is all I'll be
Too bad, To be me

Beginning or Ending?

Sad End

I unfold the saga
Of a late, dear friend,
Missing him brings memories
And stillness, in his sad end.

He dreamed of a new start;
A life without strain,
He needed a fresh plan;
A way to escape the pain.

But in times of sadness
His heart longed love,
Lonely, hopeless
He turned to drugs.

Time passed by
He disappeared,
Depression controlled him
Too weak to adhere.

Over the years
His addictions took hold,
Emotions destroyed
His heart stone cold.

Ultimately
News of his death,
Nothing anyone
Could have done to prevent.

So now, in faith
I give him my love,
I pray that he's safe
Free from this world.

A soulful spirit
Finally found peace,
Beyond this earth
Above our reach.

Four They Lay

Four they lay
As four they are,
The four of them
They lay so far.

The first so fray
As fray as glass,
The first of them
He ran so fast.

The second one
A work of art,
The second of them
Fought and fought.

The third was wise
He prayed to God,
The third of them
Knelt long and hard.

The fourth came forth
And waved his hand,
The fourth of them
Surrendered their land.

Four they lay
As four they are,
Four brave boys
Had come so far.

Four that gave
A jab at fate,
And here they lay
A bit too late.

The time had come
To face the day,
As each of them
Lay their own way.

The first who ran
Had lost his legs,
The second man
A broken face.

The third of four
Had lost his fate,
The fourth of them
Shot at the gate.

Four they lay
As four they are,
The four of them
They lay so far.

Anxiety

Drifting off the other day, I closed my eyes...
Day dreaming about my life, I realized:
So many thoughts could never be,
So many visions never agree.
Fathomed wishes; never to be real,
Instead, realities become revealed.

Harping on my discovery from the other day...
My realizations, tangled me in disarray:
My grumpy spirit cold and crude,
My soul dismayed and so confused.
Mind hazier then ever; far from clear,
No ridding these anxious fears.

The following day, I fell into a frenzy...
Remembering things that drove me crazy:
Loneliness incurred when I had no friends,
Respect I lost when I couldn't stand.
And then, there was my love's rejection,
I lost so much with no intentions.

The very next day, I relinquished myself...
Found an apparatus up on the shiny shelf.
There were so many other, better ways out,
But I decided, in my agony, to take the easy route.
Now, my existence is only in my mind's abyss, nothingness,
Finally, without risk, my conscious befalls eternal rest.

~Transition from Fantasy to Reality~

*"The dreams and nightmares we captivate in our minds
mysteriously find their way into our lives..."*

Subconscious or Ego?

Strength in Weakness

Alone, fending for myself,
Strength to carry on, no one else.
Learn lessons hard, falling down,
Taking leaps, pushing bounds.

Trials of my life, tribulations,
Failed relationships, wrong decisions.
Poisons, hazards, toxic love affairs,
Risks I take, consequences I dare.

A survivor, in this game of life,
A warrior winning a bloody fight.
Although at times, I get knocked out,
Strength in weakness, I do without.

Lonely, jaded, broken-hearted fool,
I struggle to stay alive, keep my cool.
I wonder down this path of many doors,
Choices on a whim, subjected to scars.

Yet, with all my regrets and mistakes,
I find strength in weakness, hold onto faith.
Look ahead, learn from my past,
No turning back, life goes by fast.

Adjustment: Reality

This urge refuses to withdraw
No escape to help me fall.
Lack of confidence denies me courage
I'm hopelessly alone, filled with rage.
Black visions; flashback repeats,
At night I'm blind to all- no sleep.
My heart is not able to love anymore,
I can only appeal images of horror and war.
I dream of hate and act with violence,
I lost all belief, cry in silence.
My life is adjusting to reality;
I realize, now, things aren't what I thought would be.

Taking Control

I am trapped in this world as an inferior being,
Always someone there, telling me what I can't do.
Fed up with these voices of control over me,
I'm ready to walk someone else's shoes.

I feel this hopelessness creeping through my soul,
An urge to escape, tugging at my every nerve.
No one thinks I'm able to take a hold on my own,
These fools decide what I should deserve.

Because I am a delinquent in a supervised world,
Unable to do anything without someone else's decision.
I cry knowing my direction is teetering,
Hate for those controlling my tension.

Only one way to release my pain and agony,
Beyond screaming sullenly and scratching my face,
My revenge will be sweet and straight out,
The ones who overpower me will experience
Anarchy's disgrace.

White Flag

Gushing devious theme,
Rushing black with steam,
Seeping sources defend,
Enemies scorned avenge.

Skating slyly about,
Burgundy pours out,
Destructive appetites run red,
Flirting hastily, yet scared.

Arch nemesis in denial,
Rosy cheeks blush on trial,
Icy blue attitude,
Collectively cool, loathsomely aloof.

Standing alone this time,
Isolated, on a fine line,
White flag dimly flows,
Ultimately, winning means letting go.

Teenage Angst

Hell is the gravity that pulls me down,
My silent wit,
Has me facedown on the ground.
My mortal thoughts:
Sullen-
Compelled by time,
I'm a sinner bound by my lethal mind.
The pressure of fate
Tempts me to be strong,
But death: A clear solution,
If my decisions go wrong.
Really, It's an overbearing feeling,
Of being alone that brings fear,
Although, my icy veins fail to shed tears.
Sometimes, I am inclined to stop my anguish,
I make myself mad;
With self-induced stress.
Yet, I've never felt so much pain,
My teenage angst drives me insane!
Brainwashed from this leaf of herb,
Crying at nothing,
Never heard.
Still, trying not to lose my grip,
Resisting the razor that craves my wrist.
Why do I desire it to end this way?!
There's so much more I have to say!
On bad days, life can really kill,
So, I take the bad away with a handful of pills.
But, these don't help my issues fade,
My problems get bigger,
More are made.
What then, does a teenager do?
When the world is against me, how do I pursue?!

I once philosophized:
My life was an immense dream;
With a pounding heart,
And a brain that screams.
Alas, in reality, it's clear,
I'm alone in the end-
At last, into nothingness;
I resolve to dissapear.

Experiences = World

Scalded:
Layers peel.
Extinguished:
Smoke reveals.
Surfaced:
Truths shine.
Exposed:
World defies.

Trampled:
Abrasions burn.
Rescued:
Lessons learned.
Unraveled:
Naked facts.
Freed:
World impacts.

Suffocated:
Breathe denied.
Released:
Life tried.
Confided:
New openness.
Empowered:
World candidness.

Strangled:
Bruises throb.
Saved:
Forever scarred.
Survived:
Hero rises.
Strength:
World horizons.

Love or Pain?

Emotions I

Crazy emotions
Steering devotions
Empowering notions
Stirring reactions
False connotations
Vengeful suggestions
Emotional satisfaction
Enhancing friction
Thickening tension
Constant confliction
Open abrasion
Endless mission

Emotions II

Seducing me
Haunting me
Twisting me
Torturing me
Wanting you
Hating you
Loving you
Tasting you
Teasing me
Tormenting me
Pulling me
Pushing me
Craving you
Despising you
Longing you
Denying you

Holding me
Betraying me
Deceiving me
Enslaving me
Needing you
Controlling you
Missing you
Demanding you
Confusing me
Abusing me
Ignoring me
Abhorring me
Adoring you
Loathing you
Fearing you
Knowing you

Second Guess

If our love was so truely wrong,
Why then, can't I just stay strong?
Why does my heart so sorely ache?
Was walking away my biggest mistake?
Was closing the door the right thing to do?
This taunting love, I just can't let it go!

If he's not the one, then why do I cry?
Why does it hurt when I don't even try?
Why does my mind keep harping over him?
Did I over react or was my action legit?
Did my guard set me up for a manic melt down?
Constant flashbacks flicker with every sound.

If fate so assuredly proves me incorrect,
How will I move pass this without regret?
How will I find comfort in the arms of a stranger?
Won't I feel anxious? alone? in danger?
Won't I start to wonder if he's doing the same?
My heart sinks in guilt, riddled with shame.

If time is the only way to heal my broken heart,
Do I start to date even though I'm scarred?
Do I use people because I'm sad and lonely?
Or do I isolate myself so I don't hurt anybody?
Or do I follow my heart and try to win him back?
Alas, he'll only hurt me again, resolve to let my heart go black.

The Deepest Climax (of Life)

Humble now; I'm refined,
Love, is in a matter of time.
Moments forward will define,
True love for a heart, once denied.

Passing time, turns history,
Baffled by love's mystery.
Wondering, will it ever be?
Is "Real Love" a possibility?

Something, deep inside,
Whispers to me why
The reasons I hang by:
Unfold secrets to this life.

A deepness; unexplainable,
A conscious effort to not let go.
A certainty, I just know,
Coming soon, life will grow.

Love, is in my path,
Great and strong; intact.
A lover whose heart I attract,
A partner that won't look back.

The deepest climax to come,
I am ready, for who I become,
Two hearts, will melt as one,
Finding love, no matter how long.

One of Those Days

Today is one of those days
When I'm just damn down,
Can't shake this feeling
Wish I could skip town...

Crawled up on the couch
Sulking in my sweats,
Can't get motivated
Down and depressed...

Lonely,
So alone,
Yet, can't pick up
To get this day going...

It's never enough...

Just want to be happy
Miss my love for life,
Broken down now
Why don't I feel right?

Today is one of those days
When I can't seem to smile,
Looking out the window
My heart is on trial...

It's love that I lack
Thinking about the past,
I don't want him back
I just want love that lasts.

The moments I share
Are special but minimal,
A lover who can't be there
Guilty as a criminal...

I get caught up
And hold onto hope,
I live for the moment
But always miss the boat...

Together We Dream

We dream together the day we'll marry,
Our loving bond, others could only envy.
Sharing visions of our future together,
Our son playing football, us, his cheerleaders.

Magic moments we lovingly embrace,
The warmth inside me, only you can create.
The chills I send down your spine,
The butterflies you give me, tickling mine.

You compliment my smile, my beautiful eyes,
I'm happiest, when I'm in your seize.
Days that pass when we can't be together,
Missing you is painful, it feels like forever.

Then there's those times when we don't connect,
Say hurtful things, that we later regret.
These are the times I dream the most of our future,
Remembering our purpose is to always love each other.

So let's dream together, of the life we'll share,
Always, our timeless love will prevail.
Forgiveness heals, we follow our path to destiny,
Let's be forever, our dreams become reality.

Past-Time Lover

A past-time lover
Parades my thoughts,
Dramatic memories
Of a love I once sought...

Smooth lips teased me,
Kissed me with grace,
Days forever cherished,
Long nights we embraced.

A love so powerful,
Energy full flow,
An electrical current,
A constant glow.

Alas, a power outage,
Lightning struck our love,
A crashing bolt came down,
Devastated our world.

Perfection subdued,
Wiped out, cleaned slate,
Hard lessons in love,
Spoiled perceptions of fate.

My destiny was altered,
In time, to fall again,
A past-time lover reminds me,
Love is worth the pain.

Someday

Rivers flow from these hazel eyes,
My ticking heart, stands the test of time.
Love is in his heart, infinite for me,
But I must wait, for my lover to be free.

He holds me close, endearing hug,
A promise to be with me, someday, soon.
His words are honest, his dreams big,
He asks me to wait, someday, a ring.

My heart loves him, truly, deeply,
His eyes remind me, we are destined to be.
He tells me, someday, I'll be his wife,
But, now, is just not the right time in life.

Sensitive me, can't hold back my tears,
Longing his warmth, losing him, I fear.
Waiting, dreaming, yearning for his love,
The love of my life, back to me has come.

Forever, I keep my lover, close to my heart,
In the depths of my heart, we'll never be apart.
Our love holds us together, for our future endeavor,
He is the love of my life, someday, always and forever.

Embrace

dreaming of the one I crave
craving the one I desire
desiring the one I want
wanting the one I aspire
aspiring the one I imagine
imagining the one I seek
seeking the one I embrace
embracing the one in my dreams

Sober or Altered State?

My Life

Lessons learned
Along the way,
Broken heart
Brand new day.
Trials run
Tired eyes,
Living life
Tears cried.
Tables turned
Voices heard,
Nature speaks,
Out of turn.
Surprises rise
Sometimes lies,
Selfish ways
Trying times.
Even toned
All alone,
Lonely nights
Come but gone.
Focus clear
Retro rears,
Today I see
What needs to be.
Closure stems
Breathe again,
Let it be
At last...I'm free.

Memories

If I could, flashback in time,
I'd go back to those nights;
Of laughing, love and wine...
Of fun, of delight.

A photo reminds us,
Of those good old days,
Forlornly, destinies define us,
Thus, historic memories fade.

We reminisce, without regret,
Lingering songs we memorized,
To go back, just for a moment,
Reality reminds: memories are a stamp in time.

Although, photos do take us back,
Caught up in memories, once present tense,
We move forward, hanging on to the memoirs,
Yet grasping, the future becomes the past.

Eye for an Eye

Danger lurks it's victim
Boasts blood splattered walls,
Evidence is everywhere
There's no one to call.

You wish you were dead
Your actions turn you in,
Your mind tells you to run
There's no excuse for your sin.

Shattered glass spread
Upon the concrete street,
Your feet feel the pain
As you run in the heat.

Sirens ring in your eardrums
From fate there's no escape,
It's too late, as they kill you
Close your eyes, no chance to wake.

As your bullet riddled body
Floods the sewers with blood,
They spit in your face
Kick your lifeless corpse in mud.

One must be ready to die
If they are willing to kill,
An eye for an eye
Then straight to hell.

Beginning or Ending?

Transition to the Next Horizon

Feeling my temperature rise
I know I'm descending from the skies,
Everything has gone to my head
My rushing blood flushes white skin red.
Mouth quenching for thirst
Arid as the sun,
Incoherence...
Thoughts spinning into confusion.
Pores abruptly widen
Drenching me with sweat,
Now passing through
To the next horizon.
Eyelids flapping in harsh winds
Lens become opaque,
Immunity failing;
Exposing fevers and rashes,
Body vigorously shakes,
Can't control these reactions!
Pulse rapidly beat
Heart fails to pound,
Weightless body falls
No end to this dark mass...
Soul segregates
Numb body,
Conscious absent now
Spirit roams free.

~Union of Fantasy and Reality~

"When fantasy and reality submerge, the ultimate unity enhances one's world."

Subconscious or Ego?

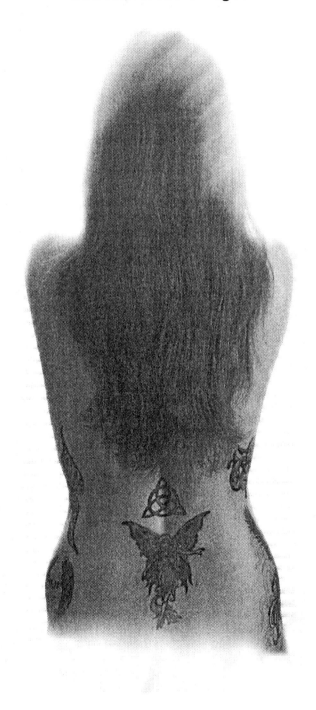

Art

the twists and turns
my life has taken
has led me to live
through vivid
creation

through my art
I express my dreams
with an open mind
one sees
meaning

Truth Serum

Define honesty
And reasons we lie
Can false-truths
Be justified?
Describe exceptions
And limits allowed
Can love forgive
Secrets revealed?
Determine tolerance
And acceptance
Can life leave
Destiny to chance?
Decide reality
And expose fantasy
Can minds clarify
What's meant to be?
Deliver response
And close uncertainty
Can society's answer
Humble humanity?
Derive truth
And question ego
Trust in your conscious
Then you will know.

True Self

The closest friends I've ever had,
Our love has come so far,
The fun we've had and secrets shared,
Seeing each other for who we are.

Not caring about otherwise "embarrassing" moments,
Reality and fantasy unite-
There is no face, just nakedness,
Comfort is justice-Freedom lets us take the night.

To my senses' furthest extensions,
My eyes no longer look away,
I have seen so much in so little time,
Experience is what makes a better day.

Novelty diminishes tradition,
Time is an essence of change,
What a world we live in,
Nothing is ever the same.

I have seen the other side-
A part of my mind where I once was shy.
A miracle which only believers survive;
Life's image beyond the average guy.

The creation of our true selves-
Although the world may disagree,
We control that creation beyond anyone else-
This perception shows truth, alas, I am free.

Love or Pain?

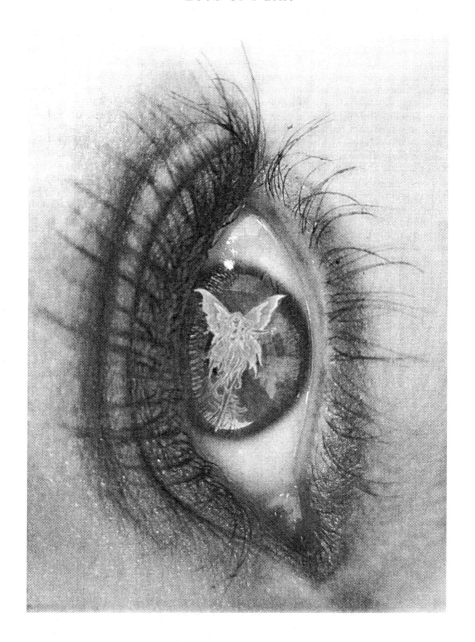

Life is Love

Love is an empowering emotion,
The meaning behind devotion.
The God in us all,
The fulfillment our hearts call.
The truth beyond ego,
The meaning we all know.
Love is an endless notion,
The sanity we find in commotion.
The feeling we find we fall,
The good times we recall.
The people we hold onto,
The memories we won't let go.
Love is the truth we condition,
The purpose that keeps us in line.
The destiny we cannot stall,
The undeniable path we befall.
The universal emotion we show,
The essence of life in which we grow.

To Find You

To find you, I had to face truth,
Change my mood, start anew.
Take the path of many disputes,
Obstacles, illusions, trials of doom.

To find you, I had to accept rules,
Detox my mind, clear my views.
Object the trap that so easily fools,
Avoid the addiction my weakness pursues.

To find you, It was all worth it,
I fought my demons, battled hurt.
Followed your voice, bled through the worst,
Suffered withdrawal, to find he who fits.

To find you, I braved through,
I sacrificed my heart, I kept onto.
No swaying now, it's plain what's true,
My search is over, my destiny is you.

A Common Fate

A shot in the dark
Revealed chemistry shared,
Unintentional love
Yet to fall, we dared.
An instant click
A picturesque romance,
Moments too perfect
We took a chance.
A common fate
Of dreams we now taste,
Unconditional love
A future we'll embrace.
A life desired
The search ends with us,
We held out in faith
And found true happiness.

Sober or Altered State?

Family Feud

Broken
From the battles,
Shaken
From the spills,
Apathetic
Of nonsense chaos,
Drowsy
On these pills.

Crippled
From the trauma,
Drained
From the drama,
Absent
Of epiphany,
Hazy
On this vodka.

Frazzled
From the violence,
Jaded
From the silence,
Detached
Of dynasty,
Woozy
On this incense.

Tainted
From the gossip,
Scarred
From all topics,
Void
Of discussion,
Lazy
On this Tussin.

Trapped
From bloodline,
Confined
From family ties,
Force
Of obligation,
Crazy
On this God-sent wine.

I am

I am
who I am
but I'm not much
to love,

No one
can see *me*
(except
for above.)

My surface
is *not*
that bad,
but inside...

Inside,
I conceal
my feelings
I hide.

God;
He only knows
how I
feel.

I have
everything-
yet nothing
is real.

When
I walk
I feel
faces.

Eyes
on me-
counting
my paces.

I close
my eyes
pretend
they aren't there,

Then
realize
why *they*
I fear...

No one
at all
can truely
know me...

Believing,
I reveal
it's *others*
who bother me.

Turn away
they dissappear,
I'm content
alone...

Alone
In my soul
body
flesh-n-bones.

Solo
I am safe,
paranoia
goes away...

I am
who I am
a loner
not afraid.

Colors

White is the ghost
That secures me so,
Black is the evil
That invades my soul,
Red is the love
That wounds my heart,
Yellow is the light
That blocks out the dark,
Green is the beauty
That nature absorbs,
Pink is the affection
That kisses my scars,
Peach is the smile
That avoids a frown,
Brown is the dust
That settles a sound,
Orange is the spirit
That strengthens my will,
Purple is the pain
That I can't distill,
Gray is the sadness
That dulls the day,
Blue is the ocean
That carries me away,
Gold is the glory
That voices sing about,
Silver is the moment
That helps me out,
Aqua is the dream
That fate bonds onto,
Opal is the pearl
In which dreams come true.

Beginning or Ending?

Lingering Memory

A lover lingers to his Lady,
Longing for lust, he lays lonely...

Through life he learns of death,
Death is a darkening thought,
Through life's eyes he sees death as eternity.

Life becomes his lingering memory.

Love's Strength

In significant loss, there is great humbleness,
In significant sorrow, there is great remembrance,
In significant sadness, there is great respectfulness,
For these are significant times;
When love's strength is greatest.

About the Author

Born in Staten Island, New York, then raised in Monmouth County, New Jersey, Nicole Cavaluzzi is the epitome of a "Jersey Girl". She's experienced the many lifestyles of New Jersey living in college towns, cities, beaches, and farms as well as working for private industry, mass retailers, public corporations and government entities on military bases. Nicole has delved into everything from volunteering with the American Red Cross, New Jersey Repertory Company Theater and Project Support Our Soldiers, to participating at art shows, and performing in martial arts, dance and music. She attended Rutgers State University of New Jersey for Communications, Public Relations and English and later Brookdale Community College for further education and career advancement in Computer Aided Draft Design and Engineering.

By those who know her personally, she is a legacy amongst a family tree decorated with a collection of writers, artists and musicians…inevitably destined to have unlimited creative drive in the arts including writing (novels and poetry), sketching, painting, photography, dancing (jazz/ballet/hiphop/club), singing and martial arts. In addition to her love of the arts, she enjoys traveling, hiking, bike riding, cooking, socializing, networking and scary movies.

Nicole is a dreaming achiever, heart-broken heart-breaker, independent, yet, longing for a relationship, both introvert and extrovert, with the unique ability to connect with the human psyche through her art and writing. She is destined to open the gateway of the neglected, unexplored dimensions of the emotional mind.